This book is for Alice.
Our brave little princess who inspired me to start writing.

To John, my amazing husband, for always encouraging and supporting me in my journey to become a published author.

Princess Lily Earns her Beads
Text and Illustration Copyright © 2021 by Sarah Bankuti
Book and cover design by Kristina Dutton
Edited by Brooke Vitale
All rights reserved

No part of this publication may be reproduced in whole or in part, or stores in a retrieval system, or transmitted in any form or by any means, electronic, mechanical, photocopying, recording, or otherwise, without written permission of Sarah Bankuti. For information regarding permission, write to sarahbankuti@gmail.com

ISBN 978-1-7778428-0-2

In a far away land, there lived a King and Queen with their daughter, Princess Lily.
Lily enjoyed playing outside and exploring the kingdom with her friends. But most of all, Lily loved swimming in the ocean.

One morning, Lily woke up feeling sick. She tried to get out of bed, but she fell on the floor.
"I feel so dizzy, and my head hurts," she cried when her parents came to help her back into bed.

The King and Queen set out at once to find out what ailed their daughter. They asked the royal wizards to help, but the potions they gave Lily did nothing to make her feel better.

And so, days and weeks and months passed, and still Lily felt poorly.

Then, one day a fairy came to the castle. She told the royal family of an enchanted forest, full of healers who could help the young princess.

Lily was excited, sure that now they would find answers – that she would soon feel better.

As Lily and her parents neared the edge of the forest, a healer appeared. "My name is Lyn Healer, and I am here to help you feel better."

Taking Lily's hand, Lyn looked her in the eyes. "I know it's hard, Lily, but I need you to trust me. Can you do that?"

Lily did want to feel better. She missed swimming and playing with her friends. But could the healer really fix her?

Finally, she took a deep breath, nodded, and stepped into the forest.

Lyn smiled at Lily. "You are very brave," she said.
"And brave children get these."
Lyn held out a necklace with a single shiny blue bead on it.
"These are bravery beads. Each time you are brave, a new bead will appear on the strand. Wear this when you feel scared to remind yourself how brave you truly are."

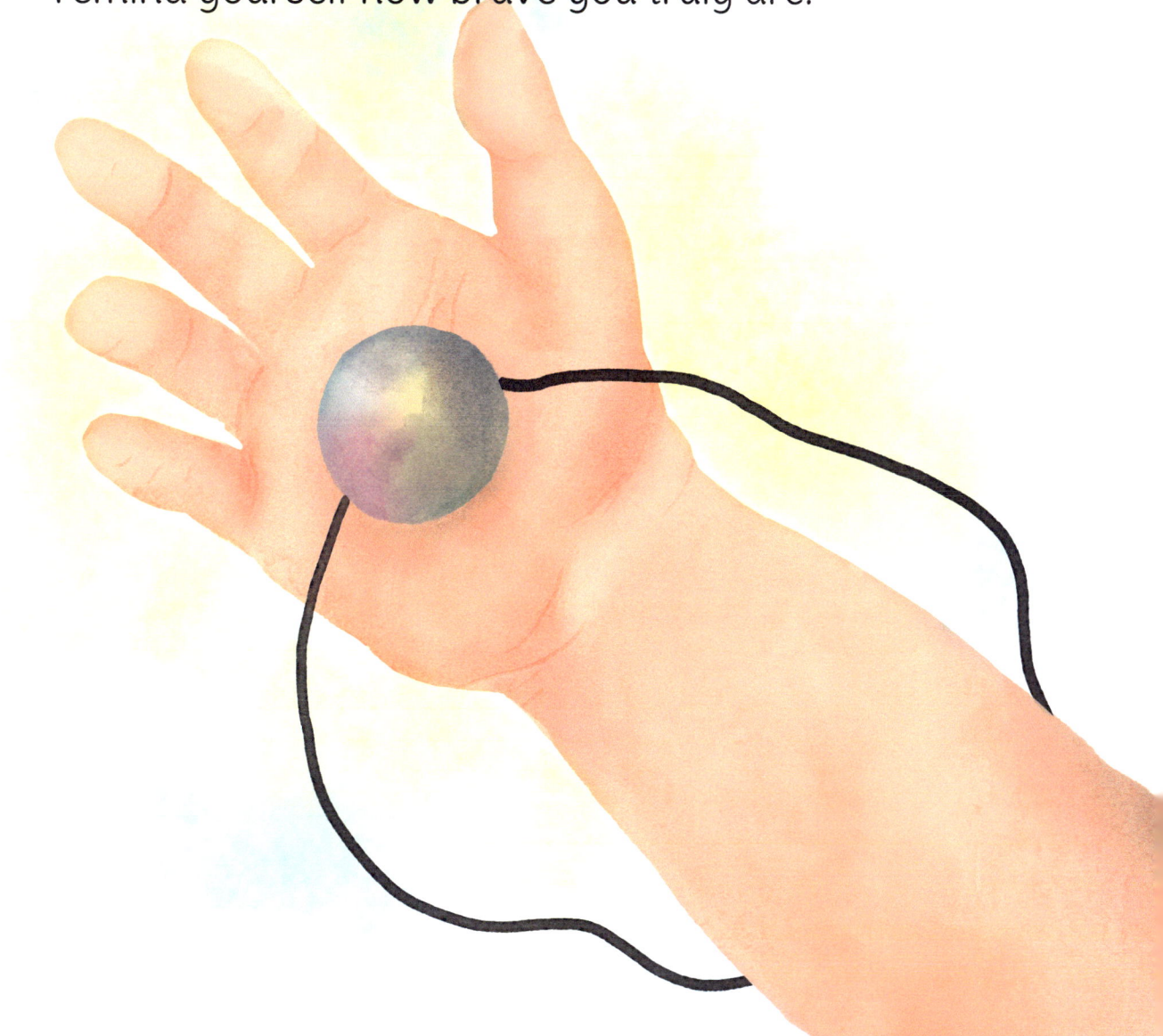

Twigs crunched under Lily's feet as she made her way through the trees. Rabbits hopped all around, and Lily saw other children wearing their beads.

"Wow! He must be really brave" Lily said, pointing at one of the boys. "Look at how many beads he has on his necklace!"

Suddenly, Lily heard a loud rumbling noise.
"Giants!" Lyn said. "Quickly, lie down and stay very still.
They cannot see you if you do not move".

Giants?

Lily whispered, suddenly afraid.

The ground shook as the giants got closer.
"They are very loud, and it is normal to be scared," Lyn said, "but remember, I am with you."

Lily held her bravery beads tight.
I can do this, she told herself.

Closing her eyes tight, Lily did her best to stay still. She focused her mind elsewhere...on the smells of the forest and how cold the ground was beneath her.
Finally, when it felt like she had been lying still for hours, the ground stopped shaking and the noise disappeared.

Lyn stood and dusted herself off.
"They're gone! You were very brave.
Come now, we must move on".
As they walked farther into the forest,
Lily realized something.
New bravery beads had appeared on
her necklace!

Lily was still fiddling with her beads when she heard Lyn say, "Ah, here we are."
In front of Lily sat a small tent. Following Lyn in, she saw a small bed. Lyn picked up a green gem. "I am going to put this on your arm," she explained. "It will put you into a deep sleep."

"A deep sleep?" Lily asked. "But why?"
Lyn smiled. "You've been so brave, but now comes the hard part. While you are sleeping, I will put a port in your chest. This will make it easier for me to give you the medicine you need."

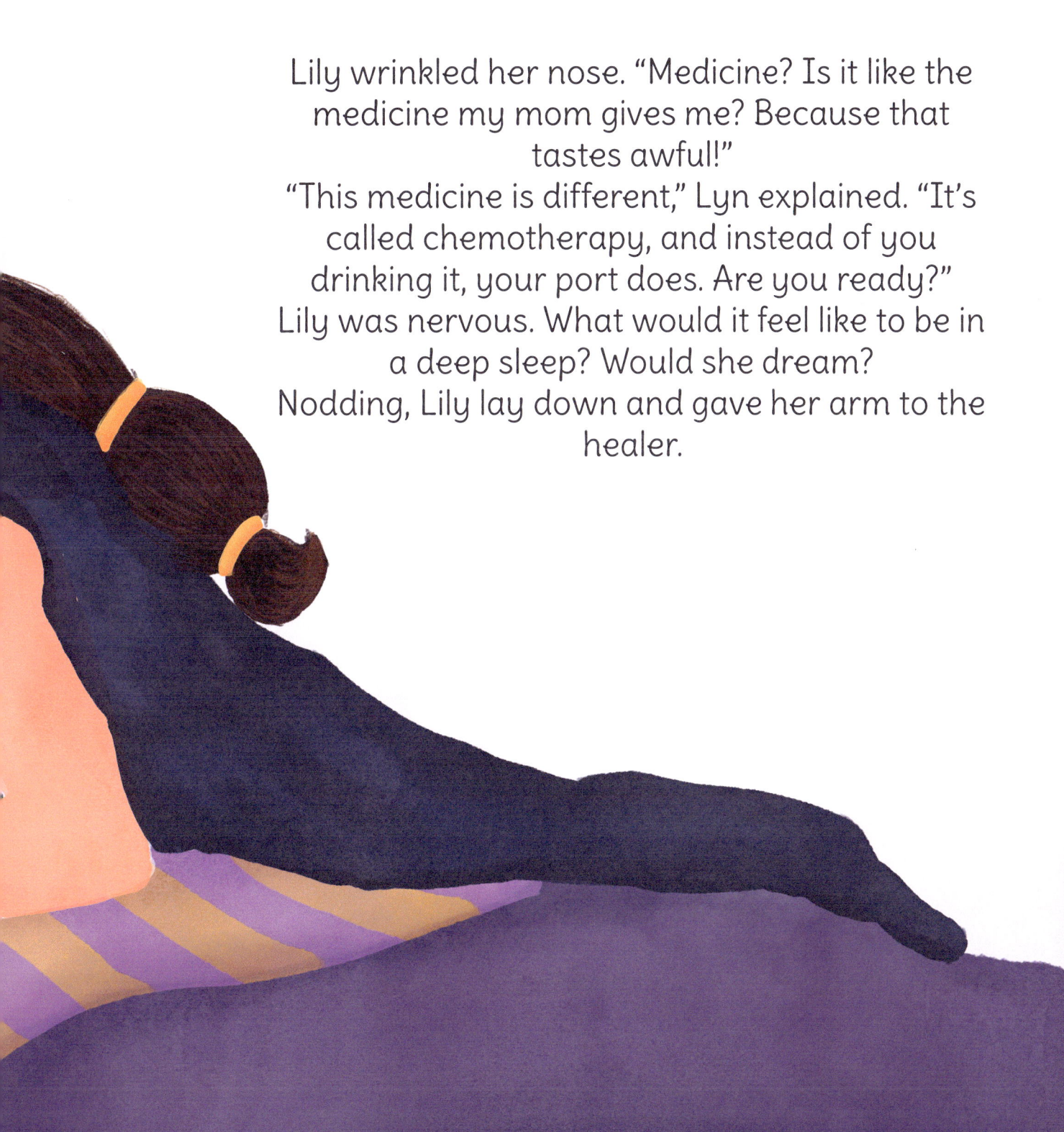

Lily wrinkled her nose. "Medicine? Is it like the medicine my mom gives me? Because that tastes awful!"

"This medicine is different," Lyn explained. "It's called chemotherapy, and instead of you drinking it, your port does. Are you ready?"

Lily was nervous. What would it feel like to be in a deep sleep? Would she dream?

Nodding, Lily lay down and gave her arm to the healer.

When Lily opened her eyes, she saw that her necklace had three new beads.

Sitting up, she looked in a mirror. Her chest hurt, and the port looked kind of funny. She felt like she was looking at someone else – not herself.

"Will I have it forever?" She asked, fingering the port.

"Not forever," Lyn said. "But you may need it for a long time. Remember, it is an important part of your healing. It will make you more comfortable when you receive your medicine, and it will help your medicine get where it needs to go."

"Are you ready to start?" Lyn asked. Lily was scared. She wanted to get better and knew she had to be brave, but it was not easy. Just then, a beautiful butterfly landed on her port. Fluttering its wings, it started giving Lily her medicine.

The chemo tickled and made Lily feel cold, but she held tight to her necklace.

Days passed, and Lily continued to get medicine.

Some days were good, and some were bad.

The chemo made her feel sick, but she knew it was helping her get better.

With each new challenge Lily faced, a new bead would appear on her necklace.

Finally, Lyn declared Lily was strong enough to go home with her parents.
Stepping into her room, Lily looked out at the ocean. She knew that her journey to get better was just beginning. It was not going to be easy, but if she continued to be brave, she would soon be strong again. Soon, she would be back in that ocean, swimming with her friends.

Lily squeezed her necklace.

She could not wait!

Made in United States
Troutdale, OR
08/20/2025

33802652R00019